A KEYBOARD ANTHOLOGY · FIRST S
Edited by Howard Ferguson

BOOK I

Published by ABRSM (Publishing) Ltd, a wholly owned subsidiary of ABRSM
© 1980 by The Associated Board of the Royal Schools of Music

1
A TOY

ANON.

Source: the *Fitzwilliam Virginal Book*, a large anthology of keyboard music copied by Francis Tregian the younger, while confined to the Fleet Prison from 1609 to his death in 1619 on a charge of recusancy. The title 'Toy' implies a short piece, lively and cheerful in character. The original bar-lengths have been halved, and phrasing and dynamics added by the editor. H.F.

2
PRELUDE
from Suite No. 1 in G

PURCELL, Z.660

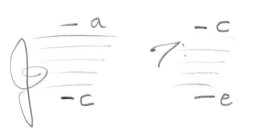

Source: Purcell's *A Choice Collection of Lessons for the Harpsichord or Spinnet*; Henry Playford, London 1696. All phrase-marks and dynamics are editorial. H.F.

3
A TRUMPET MINUET

CLARKE

Source: *2nd Book of the Harpsichord Master;* London 1700. All phrase-marks and dynamics are editorial. H.F.

A.B.1699

4
AIR in F

Attributed to
BACH, BWV Anh. 131

Source: the *Anna Magdalena Bach Notenbüchlein* of 1725, which Bach compiled for the use of his second wife. Like many of the pieces in that collection, this Air (untitled in the manuscript) is probably not by Bach himself. All phrase-marks and dynamics are editorial. H.F.

5
MINUETTO in C
from Sonata in C minor

SCARLATTI, K.73, L.217

Source: the text is taken from one of the fifteen manuscript volumes of keyboard works by Scarlatti now belonging to the Biblioteca Palatina, Parma. The *piano* in bar 15 is in the original; all other dynamics and most of the phrase-marks are editorial. H.F.

6
IMPERTINENCE

HANDEL, B.175/30

Source: a manuscript volume of pieces by Handel, formerly belonging to the 3rd Earl of Aylesford and now in the Royal Collection in the British Library. The curious title is in the original. All phrase-marks and dynamics are editorial. H.F.

7
GAVOTTE in G

GRAUPNER

Source: a manuscript in the Hessischen Landesbibliothek, Darmstadt. All phrase-marks and dynamics are editorial. H.F.

A.B.1699

8
ALLEGRO in G

RATHGEBER

Source: Valentin Rathgeber, *Musikalischer Zeit-Vertreib auf dem Klavier*, 1743. Bar 7 is editorial, as a bar was almost certainly left out of the original. All phrase-marks and dynamics are editorial. H.F.

9
AIR ITALIEN

STÖLZEL

Source: the *Wilhelm Friedemann Bach Klavierbüchlein*, which J. S. Bach began compiling in 1720 for the use of his eldest son. The 'Air Italien' is the second movement of a four-movement Partita by Stölzel. In the original manuscript there are repeat dots on *both* sides of the double bar-lines in bar 8. Those on the right appear to have been a slip; for there are none in bar 24, and a repeat of bars 9–24 would make the middle section disproportionately long. All phrase-marks (except the four slurs in the right hand of bar 11) and all dynamics are editorial. H.F.

10
MINUET in C

RICHARD JONES

Source: from Suite No. 6 of *Suits or Setts of Lessons for the harpsichord or spinnet;* Walsh, c. 1732. Four of the original ornaments have been omitted and the remainder incorporated in the text. All dynamics and phrase-marks are editorial. H.F.

11
GERMAN DANCE

HAYDN, Hob. IX/22, No. 3

No autograph of this piece is known. It is taken from a set of ten German Dances by Haydn from a manuscript by a contemporary copyist which now belongs to the Sächsische Landesbibliothek, Dresden. As can be seen from the facsimile below, the original has no tempo, phrasing or expression marks. (Note that the right-hand part is written in the soprano clef, with middle C on the bottom line.) 1st- and 2nd-time bars are implied, as shown in the present version, to which tempo, phrasing and expression marks have also been added. Other interpretations are possible. H.F.

12
ALLEGRO in B flat

MOZART, K. 3

This little Allegro was written on 4 March 1762, when Mozart was six years old. It was first published in Nissen's biography of the composer which appeared in 1828. The two-note slurs in bars 1, 7, 8, 13, 17, 21, 22 & 29, and the four-note one in bar 11, are in the original. The remaining phrase-marks and all the expression marks are editorial. H.F.

13
MINUET in C

DUNCOMBE

Source: *First Book of Progressive Lessons*, 1778. The original has no tempo, phrasing or expression marks. H.F.

14
SONATINA in C
First movement

CLEMENTI, Op. 36, No. 1

First published as No. 1 of *Six Progressive Sonatinas for the piano forte;* Longman & Broderip, London [1797].

A.B.1699

15
MENUETTO in C

PLEYEL

Source: the 17th Lesson in Pleyel & Dussek's *Methode pour le piano forte;* Pleyel, Paris [1797]. All phrase-marks and dynamics are editorial. H.F.

TRIO

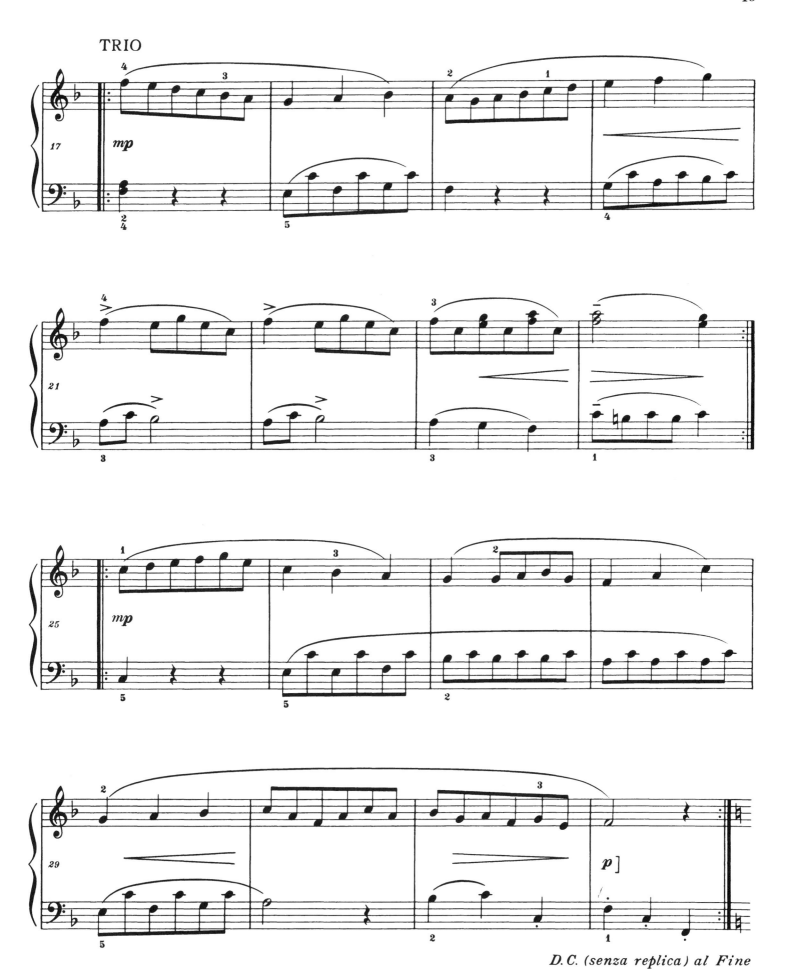

D.C. (senza replica) al Fine

16
LESSON in C

DIABELLI, Op. 125, No. 10

Source: *Die ersten 12 Lektionen*, Op. 125 [1830]. Some phrase-marks and dynamics have been added by the editor. H.F.

A.B. 1699

17
STUDY in B minor

CZERNY, Op.139, No. 98

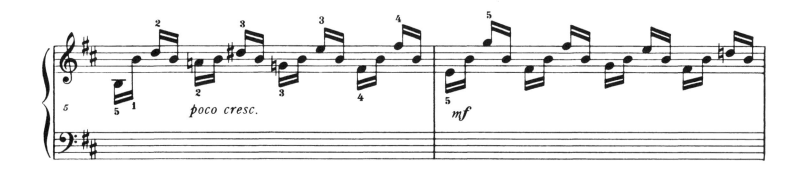

Source: *100 Petites Etudes*, Op.139. The dynamics are editorial. H.F.

18
STUDY in A minor

BERTINI, Op. 137, No. 8

Source: *25 Elementary Studies*, Book I, Op. 137.

19
WILDER REITER
(Wild Horseman)

SCHUMANN, Op. 68, No. 8

Source: Schumann's autograph of *Album für die Jugend*, written in 1848. Marks within square brackets are editorial. H.F.

20
LES PLAINTES D'UNE POUPÉE
(The Doll's Lament)

FRANCK

Source: a facsimile of the composer's autograph.

A.B.1699

21
SONATINA in G
First movement

REINECKE, Op.127A, No.2

Allegro moderato [♩ = c. 116]

Source: *6 Sonatinas*, Op.127a; Senff, Leipzig [n.d.].

22
CHANT RUSSE

TCHAIKOVSKY, Op. 39, No. 11

Source: *Jugend Album*, Op.39; Jurgenson, Moscow 1893. Mark the 3-bar rhythms clearly, and the change to 2-bar rhythm in bar 25. Unslurred notes are non-legato. H.F.

Printed in England by Caligraving Limited Thetford Norfolk

a keyboard anthology

First Series **Book I**
Grades 1 & 2

ABRSM

ABRSM
24 Portland Place
London W1B 1LU
United Kingdom

www.abrsm.org

ISBN 978-1-85472-173-0